SUCCESS
WITHOUT THE
SUGARCOAT

*Unpolished Insights
on Leadership and Growth*

Written by

JODI-TATIANA CHARLES

Assembled by the LCG Brands Consulting team

Copyright © 2025 by Jodi-Tatiana Charles
All rights reserved.

No part of this book may be reproduced, stored in a retrieval system, or transmitted in any form or by any means, electronic, mechanical, photocopying, recording, or otherwise, without prior written permission of the publisher, except in the case of brief quotations used in reviews or critical articles.

For permission requests, contact:
info@nectopublishing.com

ISBN (Paperback): 978-0-9995458-1-2
ISBN (Ebook): 978-0-9995458-2-9

Design and Layout by LCG Brands Consulting
First Necto Publishing Edition, 2025
Printed in the United States of America
Published by Necto Publishing
https://www.lcgbrands.com/necto-publishing

CONTENTS

Introduction: Why This Book Exists 1

Author's Note 5

Dedication 7

Chapter 1: Visibility Is Not Optional 9

Chapter 2: From Obligation to Opportunity 15

Chapter 3: Choose Your Circle Wisely 21

Chapter 4: Listening Over Speaking 27

Chapter 5: Clarity in the Chaos 33

Chapter 6: The Human Advantage 39

Chapter 7: The Perils of Taking Credit 45

Chapter 8: Leading With Integrity That Lasts 51

Chapter 9: Turning Everyday Moments Into Stories 57

Closing: Success Without the Sugarcoat 63

References 67

Success Without the Sugarcoat

INTRODUCTION

WHY THIS BOOK EXISTS

Success Without the Sugarcoat

Success is often sold as polish. We see leaders on stage, entrepreneurs in glossy spreads, and brands wrapped in flawless campaigns. From the outside, it looks effortless. From the inside, those of us doing the work know better. Success is messy. It is unpredictable. It is rarely glamorous.

Jodi-Tatiana Charles, founder of LCG Brands and an award-winning marketing strategist, began writing about these truths in real time. Her reflections, first shared as blogs, were sparked by real conversations, unexpected challenges, and the unpolished moments that often teach the most powerful lessons. None of them were written as theory. They were written to tell the truth as it unfolded.

This mini-book brings those writings together. As a team, we at LCG Brands assembled and organized them here to create a collection of insights that capture what leadership and growth really feel like. Our role was to shape the flow, but the voice, perspective, and lessons are Jodi's, grounded in years of working with entrepreneurs, leaders, and organizations of every size.

The goal is not to hand you a manual with perfect answers. The goal is to give you truths you can wrestle

Why This Book Exists

with, question, and apply in your own way. Some of what you read will resonate. Some may challenge you. Some might spark ideas you have never considered before. That tension is what growth requires.

Each chapter closes with a challenge. These "Ready to Poke the Bear" sections are not tasks to check off but invitations to pause and reflect. They are designed to provoke your own insights in the middle of your daily work.

Success, without the sugarcoat, is not neat. It is not linear. It is not easy. But it is real. And real is what lasts.

Success Without the Sugarcoat

AUTHOR'S NOTE

When I first started writing these reflections, I did not think of them as chapters in a book. They were raw notes from real experiences, conversations that stuck with me, lessons that hit harder than I expected, and moments that I knew would fade if I didn't capture them. Writing was my way of making sense of leadership in real time.

These pages are not about strategies polished for the spotlight. They are about the truths that surface in the middle of the mess, the moments that test your patience, force you to look at yourself honestly, and remind you why you chose this path in the first place.

I share them here not as rules to follow but as sparks for your own reflection. Some will land, some may push you in a different direction, and that is exactly how it should be. Leadership is not a straight line. It is a practice, and every leader's practice looks different.

I am grateful to the LCG Brands team for assembling these scattered writings into this mini book. They

Success Without the Sugarcoat

believed these lessons deserved to live together and gave me the gift of seeing my words through their eyes. I also thank the mentors and family members who reminded me to stay grounded in resilience, honesty, and courage, values that shaped every page here.

Finally, thank you to you, the reader, for making space for these reflections. My hope is that one idea, one story, or one challenge sparks something that lasts beyond these pages and helps you show up a little more visible, a little more grounded, and a little more true.

Jodi Tatiana Charles

DEDICATION

LCG Brands

From all of us at
LCG Brands

To the families who provide the
foundation of resilience, love, and
encouragement that make leadership possible.

To the mentors whose wisdom and
belief guide the way forward.

And to every leader, entrepreneur,
and creative who shows up in real time,
messy, imperfect, and unpolished,
still choosing to do the work.

This book is for you.

Success Without the Sugarcoat

CHAPTER 1

VISIBILITY IS NOT OPTIONAL

*You can have the best idea in the world,
but if no one sees it, it doesn't matter. Visibility isn't
about ego, it's about access. This chapter is about
why showing up, even before you feel ready, is the
only way opportunities find you.*

One of the hardest truths for leaders, entrepreneurs, and professionals to accept is that visibility is not optional. You can have the best product, the strongest idea, or the most brilliant solution, but if no one knows it exists, it will not grow. Too often, people rely on the hope that their work will "speak for itself." It rarely does. Work does not have a voice until you give it one.

Visibility is often misunderstood. Many equate it with vanity or ego, as though stepping into the spotlight means bragging or showing off. But visibility is not about you. It is about access and opportunity. Being visible ensures you are included in conversations, invited into rooms, and considered for partnerships or projects. Without it, decisions happen without you, and potential connections slip away.

For entrepreneurs and leaders, this fear of exposure often hides behind perfectionism. You wait until the website is flawless, until the pitch is perfect, until the social feed looks like a magazine spread. But perfection is a moving target. If you wait for flawless, you will wait forever. Visibility requires courage more than polish. It asks you to show up before you feel fully ready and to trust that consistency matters more than perfection.

Visibility Is Not Optional

Where attention is currency, invisibility is far more dangerous than imperfection. Competitors who are less experienced, less talented, or less prepared may outpace you simply because they are louder, more present, and more willing to be seen. If you are not telling your story, someone else will tell it for you, and their version may not reflect your truth.

This does not mean that visibility is easy. It is uncomfortable. It requires vulnerability and a willingness to risk criticism or indifference. But discomfort is the price of growth. Every time you step forward, on stage, on camera, in writing, or in conversation, you increase the chances that the right person will hear, see, and respond. Opportunities multiply when you are visible.

The leaders and brands that thrive are not always those with the biggest budgets or the most perfect campaigns. They are the ones who show up consistently, with clarity about who they are and why they matter. Visibility is not about shouting the loudest. It is about standing clearly enough that the people who need you can find you.

If you want to build something lasting, you must make peace with being seen. There is no shortcut. There is no substitute. Visibility is not optional.

INSIGHTS

Visibility is not vanity, it is opportunity. Hiding behind perfection delays growth, while showing up consistently opens doors you did not even know were there. True progress comes not from waiting until you feel ready, but from stepping forward with courage and allowing your presence to create possibilities.

READY TO POKE THE BEAR

1. Reflect on where you are currently hiding. What opportunities might you be missing because you are waiting until everything is perfect? Write down three areas where you know you should be more visible.

2. Identify one simple action you can take this week to increase your visibility. It could be as small as posting an update, introducing yourself to a new contact, or volunteering to speak in a meeting. Write it down and commit to doing it.

3. Think about what visibility means for your brand or business. If someone only saw you once, what would you want them to know about you? Capture that in a single sentence and use it as a guide for how you show up.

Visibility Is Not Optional

Success Without the Sugarcoat

> Once you're visible, the next question is: how do you show up? That starts with your mindset.

CHAPTER 2

FROM OBLIGATION TO OPPORTUNITY

*Words matter. Saying "I've got to" makes
work feel heavy. Saying "I get to" changes
the whole energy. This chapter is about shifting
from obligation to opportunity and how that shift
changes the way you lead.*

Success Without the Sugarcoat

The words we choose shape the way we see our work and the way others experience our leadership. Too often, leaders and entrepreneurs operate under the heavy language of obligation. "I've got to finish this report." "I've got to meet with this client." "I've got to handle this issue." Over time, this kind of language creates an invisible weight. It turns responsibilities into burdens, and it drains energy not only from the person saying it but from everyone listening.

Shifting from "got to" to "get to" may look small on paper, but the impact is powerful. Language is perspective. When you say, "I get to finish this report," it reframes the same task as an opportunity rather than a chore. It reminds you of the privilege behind the responsibility. You do not *have to* meet with a client; you *get to* connect with someone who chose to trust your expertise. You do not *have to* handle an issue; you *get to* show your team what leadership looks like in action.

This shift is not about ignoring reality. The truth is, some tasks are difficult, repetitive, or frustrating. The "get to" mindset does not erase the hard work, but it places that work in the bigger picture. Every report is part of a larger strategy. Every meeting is a chance to strengthen a relationship. Every challenge is an invitation to grow. When leaders use "get to" language, they remind themselves and their teams that work is more than obligation, it is opportunity.

A leader's words are contagious. Teams mirror the energy of those who guide them. If you use the language of "got to," your team will feel pressured, burdened, and unmotivated. If you use the language of "get to," your team will feel invited, empowered, and valued. This does not mean ignoring stress or pretending everything is positive. It means recognizing the power of perspective and choosing language that fuels resilience rather than resentment.

The difference between "got to" and "get to" is often the difference between burnout and breakthrough. Leaders who constantly operate from obligation eventually lose their spark, and that loss trickles down into the culture of the organization. Leaders who consistently operate from opportunity create environments where people want to contribute and grow.

The truth is, leadership is a privilege. Building a business, serving clients, developing teams, and solving problems are not chores. They are responsibilities that reflect trust, and they are opportunities that many never have. When you treat them as burdens, you miss the meaning behind the work. When you treat them as privileges, you see the value that already exists in front of you.

INSIGHTS

The words we choose shape how we experience our work. When responsibilities feel like burdens, energy drains, but when they are framed as privileges, motivation grows. Shifting from "got to" to "get to" is more than language, it is perspective, and that perspective ripples outward into the culture of a team.

READY TO POKE THE BEAR

1. Listen to yourself for one full day. How many times do you say, "I've got to…"? Write down each moment and the task attached to it. Then reflect on how those words made you feel.

2. Reframe three of those tasks using "I get to…" language. Notice how the shift changes your energy and perspective. Capture your reflections on what feels different.

From Obligation to Opportunity

3. Bring this exercise into your leadership. Choose one meeting this week where you consciously use "get to" language with your team. Write down their reactions and your own observations of how the tone in the room changed.

Success Without the Sugarcoat

> And once your mindset shifts, the people around you start to matter even more, because they'll either push you forward or keep you stuck.

CHAPTER 3

CHOOSE YOUR CIRCLE WISELY

Success doesn't happen solo.
The people closest to you shape how far you go.
This chapter is about curating a circle that
challenges you instead of keeping you comfortable.

Success Without the Sugarcoat

Success rarely happens in isolation. No matter how talented, ambitious, or driven you are, the people you surround yourself with will either accelerate your growth or quietly hold you back. Your circle is more than a group of acquaintances. It is the environment where your ideas are tested, your confidence is built or broken, and your future is shaped.

Entrepreneurs often underestimate the impact of their circle. They lean on convenience, the colleagues, friends, or peers who happen to be close at hand, instead of deliberately curating a group that challenges them to grow. The truth is, growth-minded leaders choose their circle with intention. They know that proximity influences perspective, and perspective shapes outcomes.

The wrong circle can keep you comfortable but stagnant. These are the people who always agree with you, who avoid asking tough questions, and who prefer the safety of sameness. They may cheer you on, but they will never push you to think bigger, take risks, or face blind spots. A comfortable circle feels supportive in the moment, but it limits your potential.

The right circle, on the other hand, will stretch you. These are the peers who ask sharp questions, who challenge your assumptions, and who celebrate your growth even when it makes them uncomfortable. They are the ones who refuse to let you settle for mediocrity because they see the bigger vision of what you are capable of. Growth-minded circles hold you accountable, not only to your goals but to the best version of yourself.

Peer-to-peer connections are especially powerful because they remove hierarchy from the equation. In a peer conversation, you are not the boss, the mentor, or the authority. You are simply a leader in progress, sitting across from another leader in progress. These conversations create space for honesty, vulnerability, and mutual growth. They remind you that you are not building alone, and that even in competitive industries, collaboration can be more powerful than isolation.

Choosing your circle wisely requires courage. It means stepping away from relationships that feel safe but stagnant, and leaning into connections that may feel uncomfortable but transformative. It also requires humility, because growth-minded peers will not always tell you what you want to hear. They will tell you the truth, and the truth is often the most valuable gift you can receive.

Success Without the Sugarcoat

The people you invite into your circle are a mirror of your future. If you want to know where you are headed, look at the mindsets, habits, and ambitions of those around you. If you want to grow, choose a circle that grows too.

> **INSIGHTS**
>
> The people closest to you shape your future as much as your own effort does. Comfortable circles may feel safe, but they keep you from stretching. Growth-minded circles challenge you to rise higher, hold you accountable, and remind you that success is not built alone but in the company of those who push you forward.

READY TO POKE THE BEAR

1. Map your current circle. Write down the names of the people you spend the most time with in your work and personal life. Reflect on whether they push you forward or keep you comfortable.

2. Identify one person outside your current circle who could challenge you to grow. Reach out to them, set

Choose Your Circle Wisely

up a conversation, and write down what you learned from that exchange.

3. Schedule a peer-to-peer check-in with someone you trust. Commit to being fully honest about your challenges and ask them to do the same. Reflect afterward on what insights came from the vulnerability of that conversation.

Success Without the Sugarcoat

> And when you're with the right people, the next skill is knowing how to actually connect, with your ears, not just your mouth.

CHAPTER 4

LISTENING OVER SPEAKING

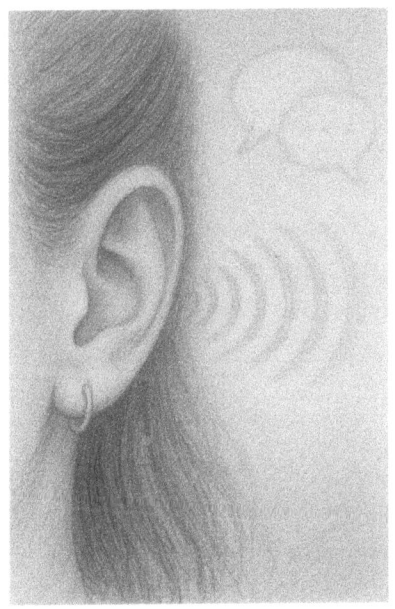

Talking too much kills trust. Listening builds it. This chapter is about why silence is your most persuasive tool and how listening changes sales, leadership, and relationships.

Success Without the Sugarcoat

Most people believe that persuasion is about talking, about filling the air with confident words, strong pitches, and clever arguments. In reality, the opposite is true. Talking too much is the silent killer of sales, trust, and leadership. When you dominate the conversation, you miss the very thing that could close the deal or strengthen the relationship: listening.

The temptation to talk comes from insecurity. Leaders feel pressure to prove their expertise, so they overload clients, colleagues, or teams with facts and solutions. Entrepreneurs fear silence, so they fill the space with constant explanations. But in the rush to prove themselves, they forget that influence is not about being the loudest voice. Influence comes from understanding what people actually need, and you cannot discover that without listening.

Listening is not passive. It is an active skill, one that requires patience, attention, and humility. It means asking questions not to show off what you know, but to uncover what the other person knows, feels, or wants. Too many leaders fall into the trap of "performative listening", nodding while mentally preparing their next statement. Real listening is different. It is staying present

Listening Over Speaking

long enough to hear the problem behind the problem, the motivation behind the words.

The truth is that people rarely buy products or follow leaders because of features, numbers, or statistics alone. They commit because they feel understood. They want to know that you see them, hear them, and value their perspective. Talking too much sends the opposite signal. It says, "My voice matters more than yours." Listening sends the message that they are seen and respected.

When you focus on listening, you discover insights that talking could never reveal. Clients share unspoken concerns. Employees voice frustrations that can be solved before they become crises. Partners reveal opportunities you would have missed if you rushed through the conversation. Silence is not your enemy; it is your ally.

The leaders and entrepreneurs who master listening are the ones who build lasting trust. They do not need to prove their expertise with constant words because their actions show they understand. They do not chase validation with overexplaining because they know the most powerful validation is giving someone space to be heard.

Success Without the Sugarcoat

If you want to protect your sales, strengthen your leadership, and grow your influence, learn to say less and listen more. Your silence may be the most persuasive tool you have.

INSIGHTS

Talking too much creates distance, while listening draws people closer. Influence is not about filling the air with words, it is about creating space where others feel heard, understood, and respected. The leaders who listen with patience and presence discover insights, build trust, and form connections that no amount of talking could ever replace.

READY TO POKE THE BEAR

1. Reflect on your last important conversation. Did you spend more time talking or listening? Write down the moments when you interrupted or shifted focus back to yourself.

2. Practice silence. In your next meeting or sales call, resist the urge to fill the space. Ask one open question, then wait. Write down what you notice when you allow silence to work.

3. Design three questions that would help you truly understand the needs of your client, team, or partner. Use them in a real conversation and reflect on the difference in what you learned compared to your usual approach.

Success Without the Sugarcoat

> And when the world feels noisy and chaotic, listening helps you find what matters most: clarity.

CHAPTER 5

CLARITY IN THE CHAOS

Chaos is constant. The leaders who survive it know who they are and what they stand for before the storm hits. This chapter is about holding onto clarity when everything else feels uncertain.

Success Without the Sugarcoat

Chaos is not an exception in business; it is the rule. One week costs rise sharply because of supply chain disruption. The next, political headlines alter customer behavior. A month later, a viral post reshapes how an entire industry is perceived overnight. Chaos does not wait for leaders to be prepared. It arrives suddenly and without permission.

The companies that survive and even grow in these conditions are not always the most creative or innovative. They are the ones that know who they are, what they stand for, and what they refuse to compromise on. This is clarity, and it becomes the anchor when everything around you is unsettled. Clarity is not the ability to predict every possible scenario. It is the discipline of preparing a steady identity, message, and set of values before the storm comes.

When viral chaos hits, the danger is not the speed or scale of the crisis itself. The real risk is a lack of clarity in response. Think of brand leaders who tie themselves to polarizing figures or conversations. The backlash is often not because of the endorsement alone but because of the lack of conviction and consistency in the response that follows. Customers can sense hesitation. They notice when apologies are half-hearted or when

Clarity in the Chaos

a message changes depending on which audience is listening. Clarity prevents these mistakes.

When markets shift without warning, such as tariffs, regulation changes, or global policy shifts, leaders have little control over the external event. What they can control is how clearly and confidently they communicate their response. Panic only produces more panic. A clear, measured message creates steadiness for employees, partners, and customers. People look to leadership for signals of stability, not certainty.

Clarity also matters in financial strain. We have written about the "price squeeze," the moment when costs rise faster than a company can adjust. Many businesses react by cutting corners, reducing quality, or shifting blame. Those decisions erode trust. The harder but more effective choice is to hold firm on what matters most, even when the short-term cost is painful. Clarity helps identify which areas can adapt and which must remain untouchable.

Chaos exposes weaknesses that were already present. If values and boundaries are undefined during calm times, they will not appear suddenly when pressure hits. That is why clarity must be written down, reinforced, and shared long before it is needed. It is not a product of crisis. It is preparation for crisis.

INSIGHTS

> Chaos is not a passing phase; it is part of the environment. Leaders who thrive are not those who predict every disruption but those who hold firm to clear values and consistent messages. Clarity does not erase uncertainty, but it steadies teams and communities when everything else feels unsettled.

READY TO POKE THE BEAR

1. Create an anchor audit. Write down three principles your brand will never compromise on, such as never sacrificing quality, never abandoning empathy, or never aligning with divisive politics.

2. Run a scenario stress test. Imagine a viral controversy involving your industry and draft a short response that reflects your anchors. Ask yourself whether your audience would recognize and trust your voice in that response.

Clarity in the Chaos

3. Hold a chaos check-in with your team. Reflect on the last period of disruption. Identify what was handled well, what failed, and what clarity could have changed the outcome.

> Clarity is powerful, but in a world run by technology, what makes you stand out is the one thing machines can't do: be human.

CHAPTER 6

THE HUMAN ADVANTAGE

AI can copy speed, but it can't copy soul.
This chapter is about why empathy, trust, and
authenticity are the edge no algorithm can replace.

Success Without the Sugarcoat

Technology has always changed the way we work, but the rise of artificial intelligence has sparked a new kind of anxiety. Suddenly, tasks that once took hours can be done in seconds. Emails are drafted automatically, data is analyzed instantly, and even creative work can be imitated by algorithms. It is tempting to believe that the future belongs to the machines, and that human contribution will matter less and less. The truth is the opposite. As technology becomes faster and smarter, the most valuable advantage in business is not efficiency, it is humanity.

AI can replicate patterns, but it cannot replicate empathy. It can process information, but it cannot process trust. It can generate content, but it cannot generate connection. These are the elements that make businesses, leaders, and brands resonate. Technology may level the playing field in terms of access to tools, but it cannot replace the human qualities that inspire loyalty, creativity, and belief.

For leaders and entrepreneurs, the danger is in hiding behind the technology. Some use it as a shield, outsourcing voice, tone, and presence until there is no personality left in their brand. Customers and teams notice. When your communication feels automated,

The Human Advantage

when your responses feel too polished, when your brand feels like it could belong to anyone, it loses its power. People are not moved by perfect; they are moved by real.

The human advantage is not about rejecting technology. It is about refusing to let it erase your unique perspective. AI may provide the draft, but only you can provide the story that connects. AI may suggest the trend, but only you can decide what aligns with your values. AI may organize the data, but only you can interpret it with the intuition that comes from lived experience.

The best leaders use technology as a tool without giving away their voice. They let it take care of the repetitive tasks so they can focus on the deeper work of building relationships, crafting strategy, and inspiring growth. They understand that technology can speed the process, but it cannot carry the responsibility of meaning. That responsibility still belongs to us.

When every brand has access to the same tools, humanity becomes the differentiator. Your quirks, your stories, your failures, and your perspective are not weaknesses. They are the very things that set you apart. When you lead with empathy, communicate with clarity, and show up authentically, you create an advantage no machine can copy.

INSIGHTS

Technology can make us faster, but it cannot make us more human. Efficiency may impress in the short term, but empathy, authenticity, and trust are what set leaders and brands apart. The real advantage comes from combining the tools of technology with the irreplaceable qualities of humanity.

READY TO POKE THE BEAR

1. Examine where you currently rely on technology in your business or leadership. Write down which tasks you allow it to handle, and which areas still need your human presence. Reflect on whether the balance feels right.

2. Choose one piece of communication this week that you would normally automate or over-polish. Rewrite it in your own words, with your voice and perspective. Notice how it feels different and how others respond.

3. Think about one story from your own experience, a failure, a breakthrough, or a turning point, that no technology could ever generate. Write it down and consider how sharing it could deepen the trust of your team, your clients, or your audience.

> And humanity in leadership doesn't just show up in how you connect, it shows up in how you handle credit.

CHAPTER 7

THE PERILS OF TAKING CREDIT

Leadership isn't about hoarding recognition. When you make success all about you, trust erodes, and teams lose motivation. This chapter is about why taking credit weakens your influence and why giving it away builds stronger, more loyal teams.

Success Without the Sugarcoat

Leadership is often mistaken for being the person in the spotlight, the one who gets the recognition, the name in the headline, or the applause at the end of the project. But real leadership has little to do with personal credit. In fact, clinging to credit can quietly erode trust, weaken teams, and limit long-term success. The leaders who last are not the ones who keep the spotlight for themselves. They are the ones who shine it on others.

The temptation to claim credit comes from fear. Leaders fear being overlooked, undervalued, or replaced. They worry that if they do not stamp their name on every win, no one will notice their contribution. But leadership is not about being noticed. Leadership is about creating the conditions where others thrive. When you make success about yourself, you shrink the potential of the team. When you make success about the collective, you expand it.

Teams can always sense when leaders hoard recognition. Over time, it breeds resentment. People stop going the extra mile if they believe their efforts will never be acknowledged. They disengage when their contributions are erased. They lose loyalty to leaders who treat them as tools for personal gain.

The Perils of Taking Credit

But teams can also sense when recognition is fake. Some leaders hand out compliments not to lift people up, but to cover for harm they have caused, to ease their own guilt, or to calm a team they secretly fear. Praise like that feels empty. Instead of building confidence, it creates doubt. Over time, hollow recognition is worse than silence because it makes people question every word.

On the other hand, when leaders give credit freely, teams lean in. They know their work matters. They trust that their contributions will be seen and celebrated. That trust fuels motivation far more effectively than any demand or incentive. Real credit is specific, timely, and honest. It makes people feel seen and valued in ways that strengthen loyalty.

Giving credit away does not diminish your authority. It strengthens it. Leaders who highlight the accomplishments of others signal security and confidence. They show that they are not threatened by talent but inspired by it. Instead of competing with their own teams, they stand beside them. Ironically, the leaders who give credit generously often gain the deepest respect and recognition, not because they demanded it, but because they embodied it.

True leadership requires humility. It is not about proving that you are the smartest in the room. It is about creating a culture where every person in the room feels valued. When leaders share recognition, they encourage collaboration, spark creativity, and reinforce that success is not about one individual but about collective progress.

The truth is that taking credit builds ego, while giving credit builds legacy. Ego fades the moment the spotlight moves on. Legacy endures in the loyalty, respect, and growth of the people you invested in. If you want to lead in a way that lasts, resist the urge to hold the credit, avoid the trap of hollow praise, and learn the discipline of giving recognition away with honesty.

INSIGHTS

Taking credit for yourself chips away at trust, but so does giving praise that feels empty or insincere. What builds lasting influence is recognition that is genuine and specific, offered in a way that makes people feel truly seen. When leaders give credit with honesty and intention, they strengthen relationships, inspire loyalty, and leave a legacy that endures.

The Perils of Taking Credit

READY TO POKE THE BEAR

Think back on a recent success. Who contributed in ways that were overlooked or under-acknowledged? Write their names down and decide how you can give them real credit.

1. Reflect on the last time you gave praise. Was it honest and specific, or was it vague and convenient? Write down what you notice about the difference.

2. Write down the legacy you want to leave as a leader. Do you want to be remembered for keeping the spotlight, or for sharing it in a way that lifted others higher?

Success Without the Sugarcoat

> Once you start giving credit freely, the next step is to anchor your leadership in something even more powerful: integrity.

CHAPTER 8

LEADING WITH INTEGRITY THAT LASTS

Shortcuts can get you quick wins, but they'll cost you long-term trust. This chapter is about why integrity, doing what you said you'd do, even when it's hard, is the one thing that lasts.

Success Without the Sugarcoat

Every leader faces moments where the easier path looks tempting. A shortcut can save time, a compromise can secure a quick win, and a half-truth can smooth over a rough conversation. In the short term, these choices may seem harmless, even clever. But over time, shortcuts erode credibility, and without credibility, leadership cannot survive. Integrity is not the glamorous part of leadership. It is the steady, sometimes invisible discipline that builds trust day by day and decision by decision.

Integrity means holding to principles even when it costs you. It is telling the truth when a polished version would be easier. It is honoring commitments when no one is watching. It is doing what you said you would do, even if it requires more effort than expected. These choices are rarely celebrated in the moment, but they build a foundation that others can rely on. That reliability is what separates leaders people tolerate from leaders people trust.

The culture of an organization reflects the integrity of its leaders. If a leader cuts corners, the team learns to do the same. If a leader says one thing and does another, the organization internalizes that inconsistency. But when a leader holds firm to integrity, even in small actions,

Leading With Integrity That Lasts

the ripple effect is powerful. Teams learn to value honesty, clients know they can rely on promises, and communities understand that the brand stands for more than profit.

Integrity does not mean perfection. Leaders will still make mistakes, but integrity shapes how those mistakes are handled. Owning errors quickly, apologizing sincerely, and correcting course transparently are all acts of integrity. People do not expect flawless leadership, but they do expect accountable leadership. They trust leaders who show up honestly, even when the truth is uncomfortable.

In a marketplace where image often seems to matter more than substance, integrity can feel like a disadvantage. Brands that manipulate, exaggerate, or bend rules sometimes rise quickly. But the truth is that those wins rarely last. Customers eventually see through false promises. Employees eventually leave environments where integrity is lacking. The trust that is lost is far harder to rebuild than the effort it would have taken to keep it intact.

The leaders who endure understand that integrity is not optional. It is the one trait that guarantees long-term credibility. Achievements fade, trends change, and recognition comes and goes, but integrity compounds. The more consistently it is practiced, the stronger it becomes. When leaders are remembered, it is not for the shortcuts they took. It is for the principles they held.

INSIGHTS

Shortcuts may offer quick wins, but they cost credibility in the long run. Integrity is not about being perfect, it is about being consistent, accountable, and honest, even when it is difficult. Leaders who hold to their principles, even quietly, build trust that compounds over time and becomes the true measure of lasting influence.

READY TO POKE THE BEAR

1. Reflect on a recent decision you made under pressure. Did you choose the harder path of integrity or the easier path of convenience? Write down what guided your choice and how it felt afterward.

2. Define two principles that are non-negotiable in your leadership or business. Write them down clearly. Ask

yourself whether your recent actions reflect those principles.

3. Imagine a future moment when integrity might cost you, perhaps a lost client, a delayed deal, or a harder conversation. Write out how you would choose to respond and how that choice would shape the trust others have in you.

Success Without the Sugarcoat

> Integrity makes your leadership real. And when you live it out daily, even the smallest moments become stories worth sharing.

CHAPTER 9

TURNING EVERYDAY MOMENTS INTO STORIES

*You don't need big wins to tell powerful stories.
The best ones come from everyday life.
This chapter is about finding meaning in the small
moments and using them to connect with others.*

Leaders and entrepreneurs often believe that great storytelling requires extraordinary events. They wait for the big win, the massive milestone, or the dramatic transformation before they share. In the meantime, they miss the quiet moments that hold just as much power. The truth is that every day experiences, when noticed and shared, can become the most engaging stories of all.

People do not connect with statistics or polished marketing copy nearly as much as they connect with real, human stories. A candid reflection on a challenge overcome, a small victory celebrated with your team, or a personal lesson learned during a difficult day often resonates more deeply than the perfect press release. Everyday moments feel authentic. They remind your audience that behind the brand, there is a person with real experiences.

The mistake many leaders make is dismissing their own daily lives as unremarkable. They underestimate how meaningful their perspective can be to others. What feels ordinary to you might be exactly the insight, encouragement, or lesson someone else needs. When you treat your experiences as valuable content, you begin to see stories everywhere. The missed train that turned into a networking opportunity. The tough conversation that revealed a hidden strength in your team. The failure that taught you how to adapt. These moments are not distractions from leadership; they are leadership.

Turning everyday moments into stories requires paying attention. It asks you to pause long enough to reflect, to pull the lesson from the experience, and to frame it in a way that others can see themselves in it. It is not about manufacturing drama. It is about finding meaning. The story does not have to be long or complicated. In fact, the most powerful ones are often short, simple, and true.

Sharing these stories builds trust. It shows that you are willing to be open, that you are not afraid to acknowledge challenges, and that you value connection over perfection. Audiences do not want to follow someone who always looks untouchable. They want to follow someone who feels real. Stories create that bridge.

As leaders and brands, the responsibility is not only to build products or services but also to build connections. Storytelling is the most effective way to do that, and the raw material for those stories is already in your daily life. You just have to pay attention and be willing to share.

INSIGHTS

Stories do not have to be extraordinary to have impact. Everyday experiences, when noticed and shared with honesty, connect more deeply than polished headlines. By drawing meaning from ordinary moments, leaders create authentic stories that resonate, build trust, and remind others that leadership is as real and human as they are.

READY TO POKE THE BEAR

1. Reflect on the past week and write down one small moment that taught you something. Ask yourself what lesson was hidden in that experience.

2. Practice framing that moment as a story. Write it in a few sentences as though you were sharing it with your audience. Reflect on how it feels to shape an ordinary event into something meaningful.

3. Share one everyday story publicly, in a meeting, on social media, or with your team. Afterward, write down how people responded and how it changed the way you see the value of your own experiences.

Turning Everyday Moments Into Stories

Success Without the Sugarcoat

> Which is why we end here, because your legacy isn't built on one big break, but on the stories you tell every day.

CLOSING

SUCCESS WITHOUT THE SUGARCOAT

Success Without the Sugarcoat

From a distance, success looks polished, the finished campaign, the confident leader on stage, the business that seems to grow without effort. Step closer, and the truth is different. You see the late nights, the rough drafts, the tough calls, and the pivots no one expected. That is what this book has been about: the parts of success that rarely make the highlight reels.

The lessons here are not about theory. They are about persistence, not perfection. They are about resilience instead of quick wins. They are about connection built on honesty instead of noise. Every chapter has shown you that leadership is less about image and more about the daily discipline of showing up, listening, deciding, and trying again.

But this book is not the full story. It is only a starting point. The insights here came from real leaders, real conversations, and real moments of struggle and clarity. More lessons will come. The truth is, unpolished success is never finished. It is a practice that continues as long as you are willing to keep showing up.

So, carry forward the ideas that hit home. Write them down. Test them in your own work. Notice how they feel in the middle of the mess, not just on the clean page.

Success Without the Sugarcoat

And when the next challenge arrives, and it will, you will be ready to meet it with persistence, resilience, and honesty.

Success without the sugarcoat is not a brand or a slogan. It is a way of leading and living. And if you keep practicing it, the legacy you leave will not be one of polish. It will be one of trust, courage, and truth.

INSIGHTS

Success will never be as polished as it looks from the outside, and that is the point. The late nights, the failures, the pivots, and the small wins are not detours, they are the real work. When you keep showing up with persistence, resilience, and honesty, you prove that leadership is not about polish at all, it is about courage. And courage is what leaves a mark that lasts.

Success Without the Sugarcoat

READY TO POKE THE BEAR

Write down the one courageous step you have been avoiding, the conversation, the risk, the decision, or the moment of visibility you keep pushing aside. Commit to doing it within the next seven days. Then do it messy, do it unpolished, but most importantly, do it.

REFERENCES

This mini-book was inspired by and adapted from original reflections written by Jodi-Tatiana Charles and first published on the LCG Brands Press & Publicity blog. Each chapter draws from unpolished insights captured in real time, then curated and organized by the LCG Brands team to create this collection.

Original writings that shaped these chapters include:

The Power of Visibility

From Got To → Get To

Why Growth-Minded Entrepreneurs Must Choose Their Circle Wisely

The Silent Killer of Sales: Talking Too Much and Listening Too Little

When Asking Isn't Listening, Power Becomes Clear

When Viral Chaos Meets Brand Clarity

Marketing Lessons from the Musk–Trump Fallout

Success Without the Sugarcoat

Surviving the Price Squeeze

*Unpredictable Tariffs:
Business Beyond Your Control*

The Human Advantage Over AI

*The Perils of Taking Credit and the Power
of Giving It Away*

Leading With Integrity That Lasts

*Turning Everyday Moments Into Engaging
Content for Your Audience*

*Authentic Growth Through Micro and
Mid-Tier In luencers*

Resource:
https://www.lcgbrands.com/press-and-publicity

www.ingramcontent.com/pod-product-compliance
Lightning Source LLC
Chambersburg PA
CBHW061234070526
44584CB00030B/4126